i

The abortion battle book

Also By Brandon Sindos

Lambtastic Day

WELFARE MOTHER GOOSE

Gingerbread house & senate

Connect with Brandon

Facebook.com/Thvndar

@THVNDAR

Youtube.com/Thvndar

δεν μπωρει να αποδεχθει την ήττα με οποιαδήποτε μορφή Αλέξανδρος
μέχρι να λυγίσουν τα γόνατα όλων των βασιλιάδων

ΌτανΑλέξανδρος η άνδρες τον ρώτησαν πότε θα επιστρέψουν στην πατρίδα τους, αμέσως απάντησε δεν καταλαβαίνετε οτι Βαβυλώνα είναι το νέο μας σπίτι

BRANDON SINDOS

Cover drawn by Laura Gillings

INCORRUPTIBLLIS

CHARLES THE MARTYR PRESS

CM

New York ■ London ■ Atlanta ■ Sydney

First Printing, 2015

Printed in the United States

ISBN-13:
978-0692574003
ISBN-10:
069257400X

Charles the Martyr publishing

"This new generation is asking for the ballot or the bullet"
-Malcolm X

To: **Sarah Weddington** and **Linda Coffee**, the two people whom by sheer force of will did more to bring abortion to the national debate than anyone else in American history.

To: **Roger Damon Price** the man who influenced my writing style more than anyone else, as well as teaching a whole generation that no subject should be considered taboo.

And to the legacy of those 9 men who were charged with most impactful Supreme Court ruling since Plessy v. Ferguson:

Chief Justice

•Warren E. Burger •

Associate Justices

• William O. Douglass • William J. Brennan, Jr • Potter Stewart • Byron White • Thurgood Marshall • Harry Blackmun • Lewis F Powell, Jr • William Rehnquist •

TABLE OF CONTENTS

Useful terms

Gloria Steinem: The quintessential feminist of the latter 20th century, Gloria Steinem was the loudest pro-choice advocate for more than a decade. In short she was the "John Brown of women's empowerment", famous, outspoken, and practically personified the new movement.

Planned Parenthood: Founded in 1916 as one of the first birth control centers, Planned Parenthood has become the largest provider of reproductive health services in the United States. Planned Parenthood is the frequent target of attack because of their limited abortion services and distribution of contraception. The controversy associated with them is made even more intense by the fact that it receives subsidies from the federal government and many state governments.

Dr. George Tiller: The medical director of Women's Health Care Services, one of only three clinics in the United States to provide late-term abortions at the time of his death. In 2009 Dr. Tiller was assassinated by Scott Roeder, an ardent pro-life activist.

Stupak/ Hyde amendments: Laws passed in 1997 and 2010 which prohibited federal funds from being used for abortion services.

Ultrasound requirements: Laws passed in several states which mandate that women must receive an ultrasound and wait a mandatory 48-72 hours before being getting abortions.

Margaret Sanger: The founder of Planned Parenthood and the person who coined the term "birth control", Margaret Sanger was one of the first nationally recognized advocates for reproductive planning, who spent her life trying to change laws concerning both contraception and free speech issues related to them. Margaret Sanger has been and continues to be a controversial icon, both because of her stance on reproductive issues and her comments concerning race and population control.

Chick-Fil-A: A fast food restaurant which primarily operates in the Southern United States, what separates them from other fast food chains the most is their conspicuous donations to far right political and religious groups.

Therapeutic abortion: Termination of a pregnancy arising from fetal development issues and/or concern for the health of the mother.

Roe vs. Wade: The 1973 Landmark US Supreme Court case, resulting in abortion up to the third month being legalized nationwide.

Norma McCorvey: A woman who was the center of a national multi-generational controversy, when in 1969 she sought legal action against the state of Texas, when authorities hindered her ability to terminate her pregnancy. If the name Norma McCorvey doesn't sound familiar you might be more acquainted with her legal alias "Jane Roe", the plaintiff in Roe vs. Wade. It would be negligent to omit the irony of Biblical proportions: She has since become a pro-life advocate.

Plan B: Emergency oral contraception that a woman can take within 120 hours of unprotected sex to prevent pregnancy.

Hobby Lobby: A chain of corporate owned craft stores that came to the forefront of the debate about reproductive issues when they were sued by employees who felt it unfair that the company's health plan would cover erectile dysfunction drugs but not contraception. The Supreme Court weighed in on the matter in June 2014 when it ruled that privately owned corporations could make decisions on medical care based around the religious beliefs of the owners, IF there were other reasonable means for those covered by the plan to acquire them.

Cecile Richards: The President of the national Planned Parenthood federation, Cecile Richards was thrust into the public spotlight in the spring of 2015 when accusations and subsequent threats against Planned Parenthood were prominent in national debate.

NARAL: An organization that engages in political action and advocacy efforts to oppose restrictions on abortion and expand access to abortion.

Feminist: **A woman who supports** a range of movements and ideologies that share the common goal of establishing, and achieving equal political, economic, cultural, personal, and social rights for women. The feminist movement has been strongly associated with the pro-choice movement because of the very strong support for reductive rights.

Wire hanger: A common household item used for organizing clothes, which is often used as a tool for preforming abortions in places where abortion is illegal, or practically illegal. Before the process of terminating pregnancy in a sterile manner was innovated, wire hangers were the first choice of any woman seeking abortion.

Hi I'm Florence

Hi my name is Florence Winters, Deacon, public advocate and gossip columnist for Dingleberry Church, the greatest Conservative Evangelical community in the world. Throughout this book I'll be sharing my insights, observations and moral judgments on issues related to abortion, premarital sex, and society's duty to eliminate both of them. I've been pointing my finger and feeling superior to others for quite some time, well now thanks to this book I can do it in literary form. We here at Dingleberry church have ethics that are above and beyond those of regular run of the mill Christians, which is why we call ourselves the "moral minority", the kind of people that actually need affirmative action. So sit back, read my words, and absorb my message...your mortal soul

I think that I shall never see

I think that I shall never see
A joy quite like pregnancy.

Abortion is for those in rutt
Jesus guide each dirty slut.

You'll know your man feels nice and regnant
When he see's you barefoot and pregnant.

Motherhood is woman's calling
Forget your career, the baby's crawling.

So I say there is no exception
Feeling empty? ditch conception!

There's a hole

There's a hole in your budget
Dear Cecile, dear Cecile
There's a hole in your budget
Dear Cecile, there's a hole

Taxing the children to death

Which of the following statements are true: 18 cents of every US tax dollar goes toward abortion funding, abortion doctors don't have to pay taxes, or the IRS was founded by Margaret Sanger as a way fund fetal termination research? The sad and unfortunate answer, ALL OF THEM! I hope you didn't think that IRS stands for "internal revenue service", their real meaning is "International Responsibility shruggers," because they assist sluts and violent women with murderous rage, shirk responsibility for homicide.

I used to think about that every paycheck, every gallon of gas, every cell phone bill, that a piece of my hard work went toward the uterine holocaust. I used to be plagued by that dilemma; either be part of the problem, I could be like one of the Nazis leading Jews, Gypsies and Poles to the gas chamber (although I think Hitler was right to hate Pole dancers, they're so unwholesome), OR I could be like one of the people who made a difference, like Oscar Schindler, or the people that helped George Bush win Florida. That's exactly when I decided to quit my job and stay at home, I couldn't handle the fact that the proceeds from my labor were preventing other women from going into labor. After I quit I had the added bonus of my husband's ego getting the steroid shot of being the sole breadwinner in the home, not to mention that he didn't like me coming home smelling like Chick-Fil-A anyway.

Ladies, if you're reading this you've already taken a big step toward ending your participation in the ghastly, uterine "purification" ritual that is abortion. I urge you to STOP PAYING TAXES any way you can. If you don't want to quit your job like me you can create a cash business, I wish we had a handgun truck in my neighborhood; it would be nice to walk out of my house and buy a firearm by just walking to the corner next to the ice cream man. Or better still, you can start a new church. If your congregation got big enough not only would you be tax exempt, but you would get your ass kissed by every God-fearing Republican that wants to run for President. I know it's a difficult decision to come to, but just remember that a dollar to Uncle Sam is giving 18 cents to Planned Parenthood, please, please: think of the children.

I don't work in the lobby

If sex is your hobby,
Don't work in this lobby.

They'll scoff at the bills,
For your birth control pills.

Your claim gets denied,
With great zealot pride.

But be careful after "4 hours duration"
They cover that hard on medication.

Cheap merchandise

HOBBY LOBBY

Free judgment

Brillo pad genocide

Do you know what kills more black kids than anything else? It's not hunger, or sickle cell, or even traffic accidents. Before you guess use of crack cocaine, crib death, or stray bullets, I'm telling you now that none of those guesses are correct. What kills more African American children than anything else is abortion.

The first oath a doctor takes is to "do no harm", yet they overstep their boundaries and indiscriminately kill black children, seriously don't they know that that's the police's job? Liberals with white guilt talk about all the deaths on the middle passage, you know that series of fateful trips that took people from repressive countries in Africa to the freedom and liberty of America (and they got a free boat ride too, my family had to pay to come here, "white privilege" indeed!), but they never talk about the deaths that happen in the middle passage of LaKeisha's legs when she goes to the women's clinic. The middle passage took mere Africans and turned them into African Americans with the same nappy hair but a new humble attitude, I would think that I would be ecstatic at the idea of a complimentary boat ride for me and 300 of my closest friends, but there were a few people who didn't make it to the other side, mostly the ones who were so lazy that the idea of jumping overboard was preferable to that of a hard day's work. But what about the children?

As I type this there is a young black mother getting an abortion somewhere, under the spell of the Liberal doctrine that wants her, and everyone that looks like her gone. Margaret Sanger talked about contraception and abortion as a way of eventually eliminating the black race altogether, and the same arugula-eating, white-guilt Liberals who think that Barack Obama is the second coming of Christ, praise her as a role model. That's the difference between us and them, they want black people gone, whereas Conservatives want black people to survive and multiply. After all, who else is going to fill our prisons?

America loses almost a million black children to abortion every year. That's more than the population of Harlem, South Central LA, Liberty City, and San Quentin COMBINED, yet nobody is doing anything about it. We go to school and learn about all the people who died to free the slaves and keep the Union together, but I'm starting to think that maybe African Americans would be better off if we had left them in chains. We wouldn't have abortion in the black community because no slave owner would allow someone to ruin his investment. It would be like buying a large tract of farmland and then salting the Earth. We would also have the added bonus of a white person present to veto any "creative" names, I don't know about you but I think "Toby Reynolds" sounds a lot more dignified than "TeShaun Reynolds", and "Aunt Jemima" sounds a lot better than "Aunt Ja'qwanda". I think I may be onto something, perhaps we could start a "back to slavery movement" or better yet, a "human property rights" movement instead.

DID YOU KNOW?

Abortion doctors regularly smoke large amounts of marijuana before preforming procedures? That's where the term "funny as a dead baby" comes from.

Stupak and Hyde

Stupak and Hyde
When Worlds collide
they say government can't buy fetal cyanide.

An agreement we can all live with,
Both 3rd article and 5th,
Uncle Sam's involvement is a myth.

Stupak and Hyde
Made amendments with pride
but people scream "planned parenthood lied"
Church groups picket and old ladies cry
because their baseless rumors just refuse to die.

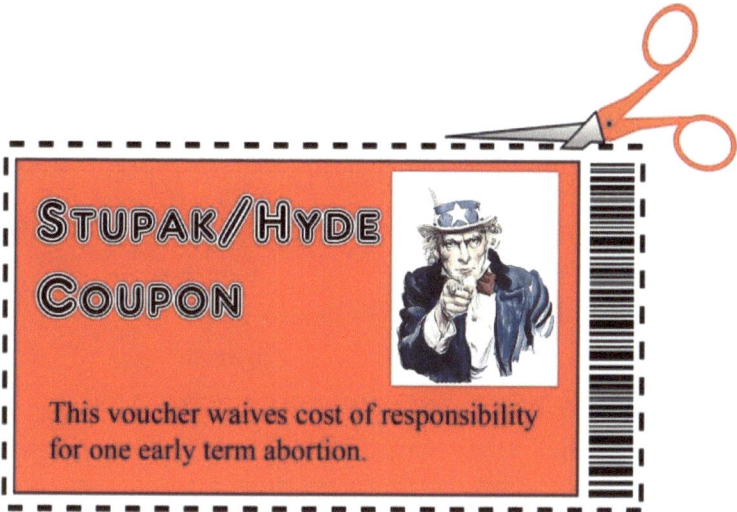

STUPAK/HYDE COUPON

This voucher waives cost of responsibility for one early term abortion.

NARAL, NARAL

NARAL, NARAL the loose girl's pal
The one who helps the murders.
Just whores who sleep with everyone
And a few dead baby herders.

Margaret Sanger went to Texas

Margaret Sanger went to Texas,
and taught the Klan as well.

The blacks and browns breed too much,
but white folks are just swell.

Is it this truth or politics?
It's not real hard to tell.

Throw her ideas on the pyre?
Go ahead, you might as well!

Pro-choice ladies hate non-whites,
It's all clear as a bell!

Think birth control pills will improve your life? Think again!

Exposing your uterus to sperm while at the same time denying it the hope of pregnancy is a cruel joke that insults the delicate balance of nature. People forget that there is no such thing as sex without consequences, if you have sex before marriage you will get sick, get pregnant or get sad every time you swallow one of those pills. If you're thinking of getting on birth control, remember this: every time you swallow one of those pills there's a small pity party, and **YOU** are the guest of honor.

It's a pity party

Why: neglect of abstinence pledge
Where: your fallopian tubes

Please: RSVP within
28 days.

Pro-death not pro-choice

I was watching TV the other day and heard the most revolting conversation since the argument to discontinue prayer in public schools. In this video a sales representative from Planned Parenthood discusses the prices that her clinic sells body parts from aborted babies for. That's right, pro-choice people have become so twisted that they're just pro-death now.

The woman went on without any emotion or remorse in her voice "$25 for a hand", "$80 for a brain" "$55 for a stomach". She went over the price list as if she were a waitress in a fried chicken restaurant, trying to entice her would be customers with her smorgasboard of Satan's business. All I can say is thank God that a couple of determined journalists were brave enough to take on the abortion establishment by pretending to be potential buyers and recording their conversation with a hidden camera. The two were even considerate enough to their viewers to edit the video show that we only see the important parts that we need to see, and omitting the extra parts of the conversation that they've assured us we don't need to worry about.

The argument is over and done with, we need to de-fund Planned Parenthood! Whereas half of their money comes from baby part sales, the other half comes from contributions from taxpayers like you and me. I'm bursting with pride when I see that my tax dollars go to the US military, they need adequate funding to pay for their ships, weapons and bombing campaigns, but the thought that my tax money has helped kill people makes me cry on the inside. But instead of tears I say that it's time for preventative action, by voting, violence, or any combination thereof; we need to shut down every woman's clinic that distributes contraception or sexual education pamphlets. Only then would we be able to curtail the amount of abortions America has every year.

Condom FAQs

- **Q**: What exactly is a condom?
  A: A condom a bag that puts pressure your penis, essentially choking the life out of it.

- **Q**: Are they effective at preventing pregnancy?
  A: Some people try to use them in a risky attempt to prevent pregnancy, but they only work about 1/3 of the time (1/5 for the darker skinned people).

- **Q**: If condoms are ineffective why do so many commercials and text books tell me to use one?
  A: It's a conspiracy between latex companies (most of whom are owned by Al Gore) and Hollywood producers who like to use them for subliminal advertising. Why do you think Magnum condoms came out at the same time the show "Magnum P.I."? So you have "safe" sex you would remember to watch Tom Selleck on Thursday night.

- **Q**: Is there any way to prevent pregnancy?
  A: You really shouldn't be having sex while at the same time hoping that you don't get pregnant, that would be like reading the Bible and hoping that you don't become better at spotting the flaws in others, it defies the point.

- **Q**: Does sex with a condom feel good?
  A: Absolutely not! That would be like asking if it's comfortable to be suffocated with a plastic bag over your head. Even if you're inside the biggest nicest castle in the world, if you have a bag choking the life out of you you're not going to have a fun time.

- **Q**: What's the wet stuff on the condom when you take it out of the wrapper?
  A: It's the extra flavoring that they add for gay men, you should avoid tasting it because you run the risk of becoming gay as well.

- **Q**: Are there any risks to women who have sex with condoms?
  A: YES, where do you think gonorrhea and yeast infections come from? The "homosexual flavoring" on condoms is detrimental to a woman's health.

Onward pro-choice soldiers

Onward Pro-choice soldiers,
Riding as to war.
Keep your heads and hearts held high
As they call you "slut" and "whore".

Take the death threats all in stride
And try not to get shot.
Hated, violence, fetal myths
Muster all the pride you've got.

Onward pro-choice soldiers
riding as to war
Walk up straight and don't look down
Defiant to the core.

Why do they regret the abortion?

There are almost a million abortions every day in America, and most of those women feel unmeasurable levels of guilt and remorse. In fact more than 85% of women who get abortions later regret their decision.*

So why did you regret ending your pregnancy?

"Because the would be father of my baby got into the NBA, that child support would've been insane."

- **Jane Wilson**
  Waterloo, IA

"Because I feel that America is desperately short of impoverished, single mothers."

- **Marta Torres**
  San Diego, CA

"Because I wish I didn't have to lie about having had an abortion when I cast judgment on other women who do. "

- o **Linda O'Reily**
  Conyers, GA

"Because 11 kids just isn't enough"

- o **Susan Kim**
  Houston, TX

"Because I was shamed in front of my whole church congregation, even Jerry the Deacon that like to touch young boys couldn't look me in the face."

- o **Sara Edwards**
  Billings, MT

There are a whole lot of reasons why a woman would be sorry for aborting their baby, but only one reason for wanting to do it in the first place: SELFISHNESS. So if you're considering getting an abortion just think about this, how you would feel if you won the lottery the next day, or found out that your rich uncle in Nigeria recently died and left you a fortune, pretty stupid right!? Be smart, **DON'T DO IT**

*NOTE: No women who had got abortions were actually surveyed to reach this statistic, our speculation is essentially equal to scientific measurement.

28

Honor Rape Baby

I heard of a practice they perform in some countries called "honor rape", where men in a village will rape the girl who gets the best grades in school, in reference to her being on her school's "honor roll". Now we all know that women who are the victims of honest rape don't have any real risk of conception, but in the cases that are more gray, like when she's wearing short skirts that practically advertise her vertical smile, she obviously on the lookout for a man who goes in hard and refuses to take "no" for an answer. As you know, some of these cases result in pregnancy, causing some of these rape "victims" think that they have the perfect excuse to vacuum clean their uterus, and suck out the baby growing in their womb. I say that we should have an extra commemoration for these little miracles, in regards to honor rape I say we should call them "honor rape babies".

An honor rape baby would have a leg up on other babies, there would be no question that they would be in stable loving environments, because women who have honor rape babies are inherently superior to women who kill theirs! One of my greatest joys as a mommy is that every time I look at my children I think about all the love and joy that was part of their creation, so what could bring more joy to those rape "victims" than to look in the eyes of their children and be reminded of the day they were conceived?

Look, rape is nothing to joke about or take lightly, rape is what the Roman soldiers did to Jesus after he died but before he was resurrected, rape is what happens when you don't teach Mormons self-control, rape is the result of a fast and loose society that gives all of us the impression that vaginas are just like holes in drywall, to be filled with whatever spackle is available. Regardless of whatever dirty and unholy thing that happens, a divine gift is a divine gift and it's not for us to question the Lord's will when it comes to these extra special children. So the next time you hear a rape "victim" talk about how she's going to the women's clinic to get unpregnant, shame her, distract her, feed her sedatives, tie her up, do anything you can to remind her that she is about to violate the body and free will of somebody else.

Confused about Rape? Use our "violation pyramid" to see where you fit on the scale.

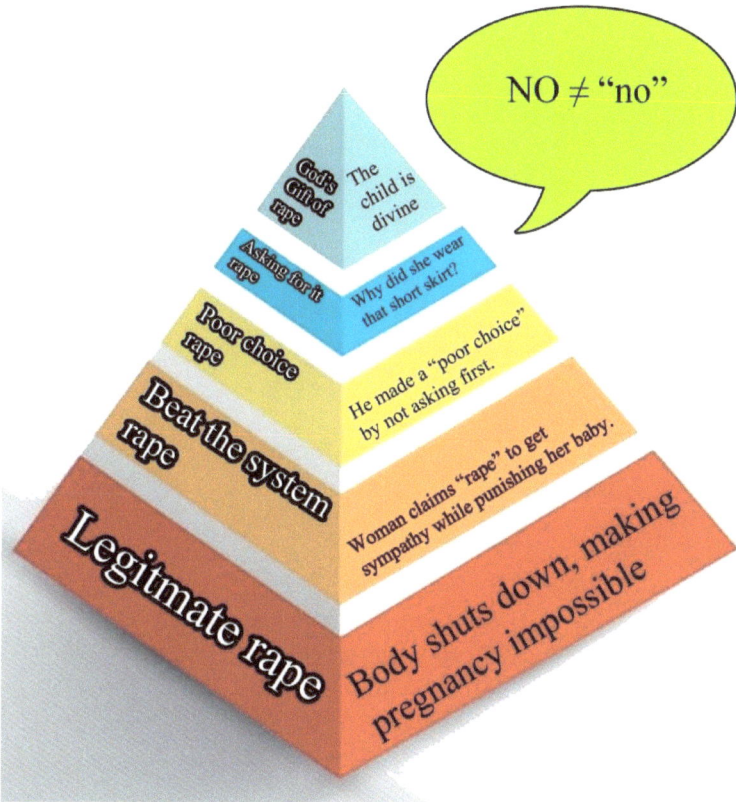

NO ≠ "no"

God's Gift of rape — The child is divine

Asking for it rape — Why did she wear that short skirt?

Poor choice rape — He made a "poor choice" by not asking first.

Beat the system rape — Woman claims "rape" to get sympathy while punishing her baby.

Legitimate rape — Body shuts down, making pregnancy impossible

On top of dear Betty

On top of dear Betty
And under the breeze,
I popped her poor cherry
With delight and ease.

We screwed on the table
Then on the floor.
She asked med for round 2
But I just had no more.

Her mother came home and
Was pushed to the edge,
She yelled at dear Betty
"YOUR ABSTINENCE PLEDGE"

She went to the doctor
And I was so glad,
No bun in the oven
I won't be a dad".

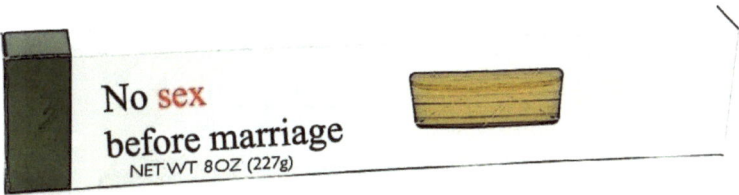

No sex before marriage

NET WT 8 OZ (227g)

The teen' father looked a chump

The teen's father looked a chump,
When she adorned her baby bump.

The two were in a deadlock
"you can't birth out wedlock"

Now no worries, she went to prom
and shook her rump
Fetus landing in the city dump.

Young McCorvey came to town

Young McCorvey came to town
Dressed like Margaret Sanger.
Threw the good old rulebook out,
Now you never need a hanger.

Incest is a CLEAN word

"**INCEST**" sounds like a dirty word with a lot of dirty consequences. Many people on the pro-choice side claim that committing incest runs the risk of producing sick, inbred, stupid children that are unlovable, but they're oh so wrong. They say that these children are abominations, but I love my retarded baby, and I'm not afraid to say it.

My second husband was also my second cousin, or at least I thought he was until we found out that we share a set of grandparents. We were young and in love, we had three divorces between us, but we were devout evangelicals so we knew all about the sanctity of marriage. We were married in

March and I gave birth to our daughter in May; she was almost a month past due. We started noticing slow development, and as she got older she was reluctant to use indoor plumbing, preferring to use the outhouse that we had built for her. We knew that there was something wrong when we realized that the dog understood more words than she did.

We took her to the doctor who did all sorts of tests, lasting days and days. After all the tests were done, he called us into his office because he said that there was something important he wanted to discuss with us. "I don't know how to ask you this politely, but are you two related?" I answered openly and honestly, "This is my second marriage, I wanted to be with someone that I knew had the same family values, family church and family name as me. I'm not taking any chances this time around". He went on to ask me why we thought it was a good idea to have children, saying that since this was a case of incest I should've had a "therapeutic abortion." What's so therapeutic about baby murder? I don't know about you, but I've never seen a picture of Sigmund Freud in a set of stirrups.

Sometimes the neighborhood kids pick on my daughter, calling her hurtful names like "Mongoloid", "Pinhead", and "George W." Whenever I hear them use those words I come outside and yell at them "leave my retarded baby alone!" Sometimes when I'm hosing her down in the backyard I think of all the whack jobs that would've chosen death if they were pregnant with a special baby like mine. If they only knew the joy that I get from my little inbred miracle.

Breeders Digest

Condoms
Just how evil are they?

Withdrawal method
"If it doesn't work it's
a sign from God"

Fertility pils
Which one is right for
your teen?

Clowncar uterus
One woman's fight
against underpopulation.

High school pregnancy tips

Hey, girls! This is Rhonda the "teen baby factory", pregnancy is a great way to keep your boyfriend and get lots of attention, but it's also a big responsibility, just because you're carrying a lead weight in your cooter doesn't mean that you get to ignore fashion rules or miss your weekly keg party. Here are a few tips that I wish someone had told me to help me get through those nine months.

* Plan ahead! You don't want your expectancy date to coincide with
prom or homecoming.

*Eat right. You might be tempted to eat from the "light menu" at the fast food restaurant, but your baby is going to need the extra nutrients. Remember the rule of eating while pregnant: The grease is your friend.

* Get plenty of fresh water. This will flush the alcohol and drugs out of your system before it reaches your baby (nobody gets high for free).

* Be prepared! Make sure you purchase the latest styles of cool, fashionable Nike athletic shoes for your baby ahead of time.

*Inform all your teachers, neighbors and any other adult. This way they will have lower expectations for you, allowing you to put in the absolute minimum in life.

* Think ahead. Make sure you get your driver's license (or at least a bus pass) in case you have to take yourself to the hospital when you go into labor.

* If someone expresses disapproval that you are having a baby at such an early age, get loud and "in their face" with lots of bitchy attitude.
A few phrases to remember: "Nobodys gonna tell me how to raise my baby", "don't tell me not to smoke weed while I'm pregnant, I'll do what I want" , "Of course I didn't use a condom, those things don't work anyway"

* Remember to eat often (every three to four hours) when you're Pregnant. You can keep the weight off by smoking more and drinking lite beer instead of the regular kind.

* Smoking tobacco while pregnant can result in lower birth weight for your newborn, making it smaller and easier to pass through your "fun hole".

* The fun doesn't have to end just because you give birth. If you enjoy the experience you can always have another one, nothing would please your parents more than to raise another one of your children, if anyone disapproves you can simply remind them "**I'm doing me**".

Where oh where

Oh where, oh where
has my Planned Parenthood gone,
oh where, oh where can it be?

The passed a law
"assure the hospital saw"
Oh, what will happen to me?

WIRE HANGER SOCIETY
Presents:
pride of termination

Celebrating a feminist rite of passage: abortion
All week long we'll be sharing stories, essays,
theater clips and short movies about the evil, yet
ancient practice known as pregnancy. As
pro-choice feminists it's our responsibility to
degrade men, society and motherhood, a
responsibility that we take very seriously at
the Wire Hanger Society.

GLORY IN ABORTION

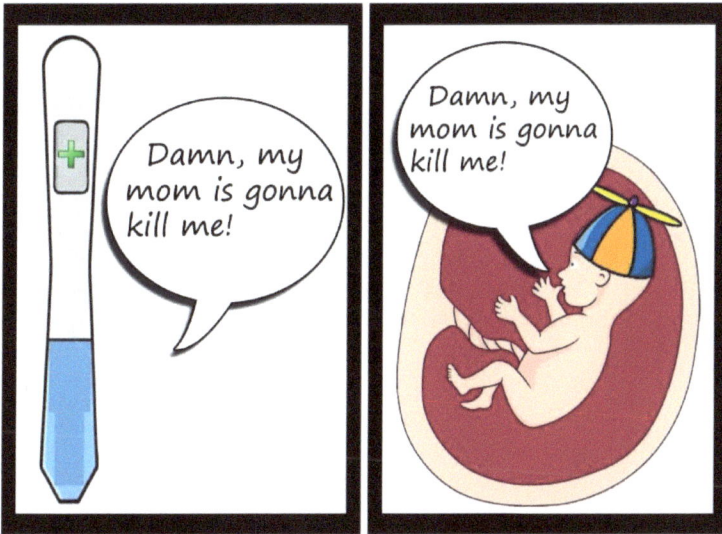

......And you thought that **YOU** had problems.

Abortion F.A.Q.s

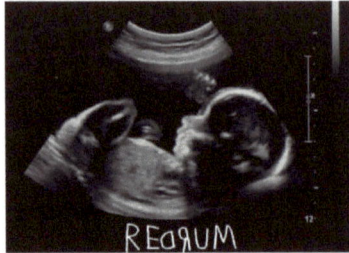

- **Q**: Doesn't the woman's choice matter?
  A: No! it's totally unfair that a woman can choose whether to have a baby or not, but the baby can only choose whether it wants to end up a stem cell or dog food.

- **Q**: I don't want to be a parent, does that make me a bad person?
  A: Yes! The Bible is clear that a woman's place in the home, as a fetal growth unit.

- **Q**: Does killing an abortion Doctor violate the 6th commandment?
  A: No! Abortion Doctors are pure evil! Jesus died for the sins of the righteous, not those who partake in the uterine holocaust.

- **Q**: Is there any spiritual deficiency in women who chooses to get abortions?
  A: There is a correlation, studies have shown that at least 19% of women who get abortions are Satanists and another 37% never got baptized.

- **Q**: There's a pro-choice candidate running for office in my state, is it ok to vote for her?
  A: NO! People who are in favor of taking life don't deserve to be elected, so you MUST vote for the other candidate, defend the sanctify of life, even if it means voting for someone who wants to bomb other nations and disregard the sanctity of their lives.

- **Q**: What do Judas, Hitler, and Charles Manson have in common?
  A: They were all abortion Doctors.

- Q: How can I avoid getting my girlfriend pregnant, and thus prevent an abortion
  A: Easy, just restrict yourself to anal sex! Not only will she avoid getting knocked up, you will also live up to your abstinence pledge.

- Q: My preacher said that everyone who gets abortions feels remorseful in the end, but I've met women who say that they don't regret their decision, what does that mean?
  A: Pathological lying is a common side effect of baby murder. The part of the brain responsible for truth telling is closely linked to the uterus, which often gets damaged during abortions.

- Q: Is abortion OK in the case of rape?
  A: Absolutely not! In cases of legitimate rape a woman's eggs will reject sperm from an attacker, it's the same principle as the kid who doesn't get invited to the Easter egg hunt because he wasn't invited to the party in the first place, but decided to show up anyway. If a woman gets pregnant it's just a sign that she uses the term "rape" very loosely.

Abstinence only education

I don't believe in lying to children, they have to know the truths about the impure and sacrilegious world that we're living in today, so I don't candy coat the dangers of sex outside of marriage. Premarital sex has led to some of the worst events in human history, the burning of Sodom and Gomorrah, the spreading of HIV, and the birth of Barack Obama. Unfortunately in the modern time of sexual immorality, sex outside out marriage has become the normal way of doing things. In the past, a woman would save her carnal treasure for that one special man who would sweep her off her feet and declare his love for her in a house of God. Now women will spread their legs for the first man that takes them to a

53

chain restaurant. In the past sex was something that only went on within the confines of a marriage sanctified by God and Uncle Sam, but since a permissive attitude that has developed among our young people new trends have emerged that nobody could have imagined in previous generations. A good case and point: 50 years ago prostitution and extramarital affairs didn't exist, now they're EVERYWHERE. So this is why I will always support abstinence-only education, it teaches kids that life is black and white, either you're staying abstinent or you're getting pregnant and dying of Chlamydia, there is no middle ground.

Did you know that 72% of black kids are born out of wedlock? YES, if there were abstinence-only education programs in sneaker stores and fried chicken restaurants the population of blacks would be reduced by 72%, that would mean less crime, shorter lines at welfare offices, and an NBA that was once again dominated by white people. Looking back on slavery now, I wish white people had spent more time teaching them how to control their urges and have families the way God commanded, instead of just teaching them how to sing, dance, and play on white guilt.

Abstinence only education **WORKS**! Since its introduction into American classrooms there has been a major change in the sexual behavior of our youth. States like Alabama, Mississippi, and Arkansas have virtually eliminated teen pregnancy, not to mention that since those states started on this course, new STD infections have become so rare that they're closing free clinics that treat them. If we lived in a perfect world everyone would go to a good Baptist church from the time they're born, and let the words of their preacher come to mind whenever they're tempted to succumb to Satan's pastime (what we call premarital sex in my church), but unfortunately that's not how the world works, not everyone comes to God's word on their own and sometimes those of us that have need to coax those of us that haven't.

Test Tube fertiizlation service

Is your uterus
a barren wasteland
of empty promises
and broken dreams?
Then come on down
today! We accept
Cash, Credit cards,
and tithing as
payment.

"Where your baby
has a womb with
a view"

Lifers are Red, Choice people are Blue

Pro-lifers are red,
Pro-choice is blue,
My vision of America
Does NOT include you!

THE DOCTOR WAS WRONG
[An op-ed from a defiant mother]

When I was 19 I was having a blast in college, I was the happiest math major in the world. I was going to frat parties and midnight runs everyday, I had a ton of friends, and my only worries were paying my sorority dues and turning my papers in on time. I was riding high on this new wave of freedom, at least I was riding high until I was forced to grow up. A few weeks after a late night visit from my friend with benefits I found out that I was pregnant. It was as if God had reminded me what a woman my age should be worried about multiplying people instead of multiplying quadratic equations. Once that test showed that I tested positive for pregnancy I put aside radical feminist concepts like "career", "education" and "independence", and focused on what matters.

The whole thing was a trial by fire from the start, I had never seen my parents so angry and disappointed, they had high hopes of me being married before having children, but their hopes of me avoiding the abortion table at all costs were more important. The father couldn't care less, talking about how he didn't even remember the night that the baby was conceived "I only use condoms, are you sure it was me that knocked you up", of course it was him he was the only one that never pulls out. He made it clear that even if the baby was his he wasn't going to be a part of the project, so I did the only rational thing I could do, dropped out of school and moved back in with my parents. It was an adjustment at first, but when I started going to my doctor visits I got used to being back home.

When I found out that I was going to have a girl I named her Evelyn, after my grandmother who was the first in our family to attain an Mrs. degree. It was during the 2nd trimester, when I was preparing the baby nursery in my parents basement, that the doctor called and told me that he suspected there may be a problem and that I needed to take a series of tests.

After the tests the doctor sat me down and told me that my baby had "Trisomy 13", a rare disease that inevitably leads to premature death. His uncaring, cold blooded words still haunt me, "the baby won't live more than four days, I recommend getting a *therapeutic abortion*". I was shocked to hear those words, how could anyone be so callous, and forget that the hand of God works in all things? I ignored his words of discouragement, and went on ahead and had my baby, and you know what? I was so glad that I did!

The doctor said that I would only have four days with my little keg night miracle, but I knew that he was wrong, I knew that this baby would overcome the words spoken over her. Day four passed, then day five, she ended up living almost a whole three weeks. I went up to the doctor after those 20 days, with my head held high and boastfully yelled in his face **IT SEEMS YOU WERE WRONG**. He was off by almost 2 weeks, looks like I showed him! Some people try to tell me that the baby knew nothing but pain its whole life and that termination was the "humane thing", that may be true, but I didn't have any guilt and that's what's most important.

Since then I've been on the pro-life circuit, telling other young women my story so I can share the only equation that I need these days, Faith > Science. Nothing makes me smile like meeting girls who used to be like me and have since gone on to the most noble profession a woman could possibly have: MOMMY. I'm proud to say that while I was writing this I just got a email from yet another girl who's decided to drop out and dedicate her life motherhood, yeah she was the first person in her family to go to college, but she's also the first person in her family to get baby shower gifts from a luxury boutique, so it balances out. So, to little Evelyn in heaven, you should know this, thanks to you mommy has the moral high ground and commands the respect of teen moms everywhere, mommy may have dropped out of college, but she can still feel superior to a lot of women who didn't, **thank you**.

WIRE HANGER SOCIETY
honor in abortion

PREGNANCY IS THE "ULTIMATE STD" RALLY

UNION SQUARE, NYC JAN 22

Join us as we rally to fight against our maternal
inclinations. and demonize motherhood. We
women have been suffering through pregnancy
for generations and have nothing to show for
it (besides the perpetuation of the human race).
Let's let our voices be heard in unison as we
bared homemakers, baby sitters, and those
that use their vaginas for anything but orgasms.

I'm in your face with feminism

I'm a feminist! That's a strong, in your face word, but I'm a strong in your face kind of woman. I'm a feminist, I'm here to wreck your societal norms, destroy tradition, and put men in their place. I'm a feminist and I'm coming for you, your church, your school, and if I have time I'll come for your guns and daughter's virginity as well.

I think my first foray into feminism was when I was eight. Mr. Gency, the principal at my elementary school, asked me to tie my shoes so that I don't trip and hurt myself. I was going to at first, but then I realized that I would be caving in to a male authority figure, and I couldn't do that. So in an act of feminist defiance I let my laces go even looser, screaming "you can't tell me what to do Mr. Gency, I won't cower in the face of your penile oppression", and paraded down the hallway to the stairs. Yeah sure, I did trip and fall like he warned me about, and yeah I need 17 stitches in my face, but I showed him: Kate Bonnel takes orders from NO MAN!

The spirit of feminism continued to grow inside me as I got older. Around the time I was 16 I stopped shaving. Nature didn't dictate that women should look like Mr. Clean downstairs, male dominated society did. To stand out among the other feminists at high school I also stopped washing, because a natural vagina is a happy vagina, and I had no intention of going through life with a depressed snatch. Why should I have to take Prozac for my cunt (we're taking back that word) just so I can appease a man who should be grateful for the privilege of pleasing my lady bits in the first place? It's those whom are willing to go the extra mile that stand out in life, and that was definitely me.

I looked, smelled and even tasted like a feminist, and all the other girls in the Norma McCorvey High School feminist society (before it was known as the Wire Hanger society) recognized me as their leader because of it. This was great and all, but I was still nervous and excited about going to college so I could finally perform the ultimate feminist rite.

I got pregnant when I was 19, a natural result of being taught about condoms and birth control when I was in high school, I heard the word "sex ed" and immediately assumed that adults were encouraging me to be promiscuous. When I was a freshman at at Norma McCorvey High School they were going to start an abstinence only education program, but all the abortion doctors in our town fought against the measure and defeated it, because if people practice abstinence they can't get abortions. When I tested positive for pregnancy I knew that I had only had two choices, either get an abortion -OR- get an abortion and brag about it. It took me less than three minutes to make a decision.

When I arrived at the women's clinic I renounced Jesus and acknowledged Satan, bragged about how many men I'd slept with, and discussed a price that we would try to auction off the aborted baby parts for, but you know all standard procedures, I don't have to tell you. When I left I had an ear to ear grin on my face, not only was I free to go out and have sex with random strangers again, but I was also part of the "termination club", so when my girlfriends would brag about their abortions I wouldn't feel like I was outside of the clique. The level of confidence you feel after murdering someone and getting away with it is ten times greater than winning a gold medal in the Olympics, the fact that I murdered someone legally and openly, and at the cost of the US taxpayer, made it that much greater. After that I knew that I could do anything

After that I was a woman without boundaries, there was nothing that I wouldn't do to show the natural superiority of women. This culminated in my four year lesbian phase, when I only dated and slept with women, my favorite women to date were illegal Hispanic immigrants, not only did it offend my grandmother and all of her Christian Scientist friends, but it also gave me a legitimate excuse to be offended at the words of Conservative white people that said things that I disagreed with. Eventually I stopped being a lesbian because I moved to Manhattan where nobody cares, and if I'm not offending someone or claiming status as a victim, what is the point of dating women???

Ladies if you learn nothing else from my words on this subject, remember this: Abortion makes you strong, it gives you power that you never knew you had, and turns you into a proud, confident person. Are you worried about going to college, starting a business, competing with men ect? Go out and have an abortion, getting pregnant is fun, easy and often includes free food and/or alcohol, and getting an abortion is also cheap and easy, they're paid for by the government and often result in receiving free gifts and raffle prizes. Just go out and do it now, you can thank me later, when you're too indifferent and desensitized to be phased by an ultrasound, disapproving man, or hormonal inclination to reproduce.

-   Kate "The Terminator" Bonnel

Did you know:

Emergency contaception A.K.A. "plan B", can cause lethargy, depression and even suicidal feelings?

That's why it's commonly called the *"mourning after"* pill.

This has been a message from the **Moral Minority**

Oh dear Nana

Oh, I come from Alabama with a shotgun by my knee
going to Louisiana, so the unwed moms can see.
The fools and poli'tcians say, you need no ultrasound
I won't stop till, my eyes have seen them all burnt to
the ground.

Oh dear Nana! Oh don't you cry for me!
I come from Alabama with a shotgun by my knee.

I went to women's clinics with my firearm in hand
They'll rue the day they heard the phrase
that Parenthood was Planned.
I gave them each a bullet with their
Last and Christian names
They'll sleep with Satan every night under warmth of
hades flames.

Oh dear Nana! Oh don't you cry for me!
I come from Alabama with a shotgun by my knee.

My trial was a drama show with folks from all the land,
They tried to call me "murderer"
why don't they understand?
They praise the girls who are a mom,
but never are a wife,
But point their fingers, and raise their voice,
when I save a baby's life!

Oh dear Nana! Oh don't you cry for me!
I come from Alabama with a shotgun by my knee.

They gave me life behind these bars
in the peni'tentiary.
I get congrats and words of praise,
from people sea to sea.
I'm glad I did my part to fight the war of Satan's strife,
I'm like John Brown of yesteryear, I saved a baby's
life.

Oh dear Nana! Oh don't you cry for me!
I come from Alabama with a shotgun by my knee.

You are an amazing
defender of life!
Even John Brown wasn't
as heroic as
you are. God bless you,
and keep the
faith.

- Joni Ernst

My daughter asked me

My daughter came up to me yesterday using a dirty word that was too adult for her. She approached me asking "Mommy what's abortion? I heard that 'strong independent women' can get them without feeling guilty. I want to be a strong independent woman when I grow up, so maybe I should get an abortion also." I was flabbergasted, how could my sweet and innocent little girl, who was so smart that she knew the difference between a Mexican and a pedophile at the age of six, come to me with such disgusting language and ideas, "strong independent woman", really? I tried to keep calm and maintain my composure, asking her where she had heard these impure concepts. Her response was a wakeup call about some of my failures as a parent: "The Hillary Clinton lady said it on TV", and after that I just lost it, but in a good way though.

I did what any other rational parent would do, I beat her senseless! What other way is there to teach her that violence against children is wrong, which is what abortion is. I gave her some much needed discipline then went upstairs to wash the blood off the curling iron, after that I came back downstairs to explain to her why all the things she said were wrong. In my soft, post assault and battery voice, I stated from the beginning "Honey, your first mistake was to want to be an 'independent woman', the only kind of women who don't need a man are lesbians, do you think your friends would invite you to their sleepovers and pool parties if your breath smelled like sushi all the time? I don't think so!"

I went on, just to make sure she got the whole message "Abortion is a crime against God, only sluts, rabid chimpanzees, and Lutherans get them. Remember: no good cook takes a bun out of the oven before its ready."

I haven't pat myself on the back in a long time, mostly because it's still sore from when my husband kicked me in the spine a few times last month, but today I made an exception. I was a good mommy, not only did I teach my little girl the evils of abortion, but I also taught her the most fundamental law of Christianity and women who get an abortion: Don't forgive them for they DO know what they do.

Old Dr. Tiller

There was an old Dr named Tiller
In his community he was a Pillar.
But Schroeder became a divine herder,
yelling "Thou shalt not murder"
With his trial being an abortion thriller.

Moral Minority

pro-life-action awards nominees

Spencer Crockett Killed his girlfriend Kim with a baseball bat after she had an abortion, lied about it and tried to excuse her behavior by saying "It's my body and you can't tell me what to do with it". Well that's 3 strikes for you Kim, YOU'RE OUT.

Agnes McNeil meticulously stalked an abortion doctor for six weeks, learning his schedule, his habits, and the dimensions of his home. Her attention to detail paid off when she surprised him in his backyard one brisk October night and choked him to death with the umbilical cord of an aborted baby. As a child Agnes was always taught to repurpose used items, so instead of throwing umbilical cord away, she used it to feed the doctor justice.

To give an abortion doctor a taste of his own medicine, **Britany Sneedler** stuffed Dr. Harry McCorey in a tight warm bag and stabbed him in the heart with a sterile knife. Don't feel sorry for Dr. McCorey though, he could've been stabbed with a dirty coat hanger.

After learning that his girlfriend Allison had an abortion without his express written consent, **Jimmy Colson** thought of the perfect way to get even with her. While she was out Jimmy dipped her vibrator in industrial strength glue and chili powder and waited for the magic to happen. Her cries of vaginal pain were like music to his ears, knowing that her means of carnal pleasure had become the source of pain. Here's a tip Allison: if you insist on masturbating, find a good seeing eye dog first.

Cast you ballot via text, e-mail, or spiteful prayers.

Sticks and stones

Sticks and stones may break my bones
And pro-choice words will hurt me.
They speak with "women's freedom" tones
But their clinic does alert me

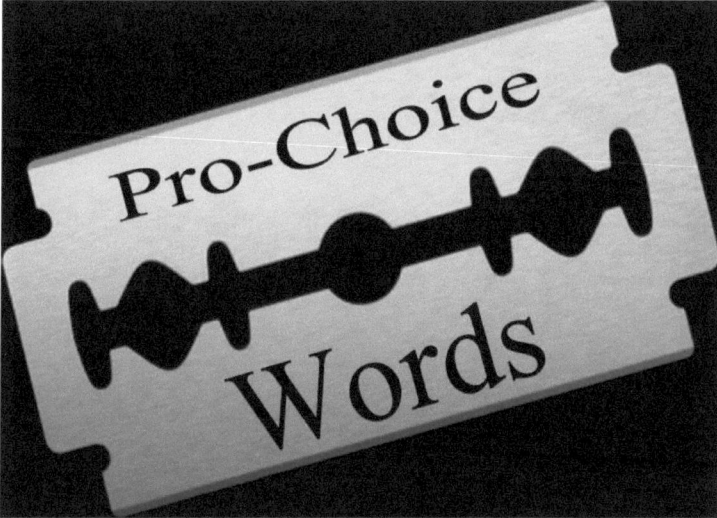

Pro-Choice Words

When Liberals are pro-life

Left wing extremists are a very hypocritical bunch that are pretty inconsistent with their standards. They talk about freedom of religion, but they deny my religious freedom to stop gays and Mormons from exercising theirs, they march for freedom of speech but are quick to shout down anyone who contradicts their lies about climate change, they talk about oppression yet feel free to oppress white males to the point of making them a marginalized, powerless and voiceless segment of society. But the worst is their double standard on abortion.

Those who scream bloody murder about a woman's right to "choose" (I'm still confused how a baby is a "choice"), the ones who say aborting a child with Down syndrome or mental retardation is a "no brainer" (I don't know if their pun is intended), are the ones who oppose abortion when a pro-life stance suits their socialist goals. I'm as pro-life as they come, in fact, I'm so pro-life that I advocate the death penalty for anyone involved in the abortion industry, but if I had to choose which children would be getting aborted it definitely wouldn't be the children that go to school, pizza parties, and soccer practice with mine.

Liberals have a bleeding heart when it comes to Anchor babies. That may be a not so nice term for babies born on American soil just so their mothers can stay here and collect welfare, but me having to pay for their socialist entitlements isn't so nice either. Yeah, it may be true that I don't pay taxes because I'm on disability and collect unemployment, but at least I'm not benefitting from any government programs, anyway, when other people I know do pay taxes for those people it gets me just as riled up as if it were me paying.

When we talk about letting patriots get on the border wall and shoot people trying to illegally enter our country, suddenly they develop a conscience and are concerned with human rights and the sanctity of life. When Lefties see illegal immigrants come here and have children they know they're adding names to the list of gullible fools, who are only too eager to cast their vote for the next person to offer free stuff paid for with other people's hard earned money. A baby that might grow up to be a God fearing, gun loving American is disposable in their view, but a baby that could grow up to spend their life blaming native born white people for all their problems, while at the same time living off them, is a treasure. That's why you never see abortion clinics in Hispanic neighborhoods, but Conservative white neighborhoods have one on every corner, many even have more abortion centers than they have McDonalds.

I think the only way to compromise this issue is to make sure that those who want them here are the ones responsible for them. We can tax things like Starbucks and stores that sell bongs and rolling papers, the types of places that Liberals love but Conservatives avoid like the plague, to pay for the social benefits that illegal immigrants get. Instead of government vouchers for housing, they can just stay with the people who argue that they're not ruining America, I'm sure little Suzy tree hugging college student could make a little space in her dorm room for Manuel from Guatemala. With the kind of laws that make left leaning people responsible for their own demands, instead of burdening others to pay for the freebies they like, it would only be a matter of time before they realized how wrong they are, and we could take steps to make America immigrant free, just like how the pilgrims envisioned it.

Our country is dying

Our country is dying,
Our morals are dead.
What these feminists need
Is a trip to the shed.

The meaning

The 1992 Presidential election was a milestone for a multitude of reasons. Not only was it the first election that I followed closely, but it was also the catalyst for a lot of discussion about "adult topics" like infidelity and drug use (or disuse?) One of my fondest memories from that election cycle was the moment that Bill Clinton was the declared the winner, because it was in that instant that the deep depression that my grandmother entered when Michael Dukakis lost finally began to lift.

What was most poignant about that election was that it was my first real introduction to the controversy surrounding abortion. Seemingly every school day of that year my teacher Mrs. Grossbach, would rail about how she felt that a woman's right to choose was a matter of common sense, then after coming home I would watch TV and get exposed to infomercials with Charlton Heston discursively describing the procedure for termination of a pregnancy. This was contrasted against the rhetoric of people like Gloria Steinem who equated being pro-life with being pro-slavery.

Before that fateful election I knew what abortion was, but I wasn't aware of the controversy or strong emotions connected to it, but after that it seemed to come up more and more frequently as I stepped further and further away from the "innocence of childhood." Even prominent religious figures both made references to the Bible to prove that their side was the righteous one.

I will make breath enter you, and you will come to life.
- Ezekiel 37:5

Before I formed you in the womb, I knew you.
- Jeremiah 1:5

The controversy eventually hit home when it presented itself within my own family. I remember the day I turned 15. I remember my grandmother called to wish me a happy birthday and in the course of our conversation we went on one tangent that eventually led us to the topic of reproductive issues, she went on a diatribe, describing abortion as an act which is morally repugnant and inexcusable. Then, several hours later when my grandfather called to give me his regards as well, we also got on topic of sex and unplanned pregnancy. I don't think it would be possible for me to ever forget the words he spoke to me "you're getting of age when you might run into 'adult problems', I hope you're practicing safe sex but if you get your girlfriend pregnant call me and I'll pay for the abortion, it'll be between us, your parents don't need to know".

I think that it was after that day of conflicting messages that I resolved myself to write about reproductive issues one day, if this controversy could be so visible and vigorous in a family, it's easy to see how vitriol comes so readily between strangers who fight over this matter. When one sees their side's victory as essential for the survival of civilization, harsh words, dramatic action, and even death or the threat thereof are alarming at first but become a logical consequence after one is exposed to the contention long enough. Abortion is the most controversial issue America has had since slavery, and unlike the slavery issue which was settled after the passing of the 13th amendment, Roe vs. Wade was just the beginning. Even the element of mistruth surrounding the matter reaches levels unmatched by any other issue, which is remarkable considering that blatant lying in the political arena is as American as apple pie. Although the topic of abortion is ever present in the American political consciousness, the issue was brought back to the forefront of discussion in the spring of 2015 when a video emerged on the internet that allegedly shows a representative from Planned Parenthood discussing the organization's efforts to make profits by selling body parts of aborted fetuses.

Although the video was proven to be heavily doctored, omitting large parts of the conversation as well as the context of each statement, most people who were outraged by the video didn't alter their words or behavior after the found out that the video had been faked, prioritizing their raw emotions over objective facts.

The firestorm of controversy was further incited when many politicians running for President in the 2016 election cycle used the video as evidence that their stance on women's health clinics was correct all along and these clinics should lose their non-profit status, all government subsidies, and potentially be criminally investigated. While some in the media did their due diligence and questioned the candidates ability to discern fact from fiction, many other news outlets amplified their message, casting people who work in contraceptive clinics as accomplices to murder. If no other idea is conveyed in the book it should be this: No matter who the next President, Supreme Court Justice, Media Mogul or public face of reproductive issues is, this controversy which has gone on since the advent of written language has no end in sight, if history is any indication of the future, one should expect us to be fighting this exact same battle 1,000 years from now.

- Brandon Thvndar Sindos

Acknowledgements

This acknowledgement section would be lacking if I didn't first recognize the words of Claire Forde, who allayed my doubts and convinced me to write this book, acting as a voice of courage, creativity and encouragement throughout the entire process.

I also have to give an extra special thanks to Laura Gillings for volunteering her immense talent and imagination to making the cover drawing, knowing the vision I had and then taking it to a new level, and at breakneck speed at that. Laura has a meteoric creative career ahead of her and I'm honored that I got to be a part of it.

Where is an author without a copy editor? Lost, that's where! Thanks to Elizabeth Jarvis for being such a fast, efficient and humorous editor.

Next a shout out to those who were always available to review concepts and ideas Amanda Jordan (who gave her perspective as a fellow writer) and "Yumi" Malik (who never accepted anything but my absolute best). People like them make the work of a writer much easier and far more rewarding.

I would be remiss if I didn't also acknowledge my 5th grade teacher Mrs. Frayda Grossbach, who was the first adult that I ever engaged in detailed discussion about abortion issues with. Although I'm glad that at home I got a 100% truthful education about abortion, receiving empirical, scientific, medical textbook explanations about the subject, Mrs. Grossbach discussed the charged emotions attached to the issue, teaching us to be courageous with our words on the subject.

Another acknowledgment I have to make it that of the legacy of Theodor Geisel A.K.A. "Dr. Seuss", whose stories filled me with wonder and ambition. Reading his books that used rhyming words and colorful illustrations to touch upon a wide range of subjects made me want to imitate him. It was his publication "The butter battle book" that served as the inspiration for the title of this one. Unquestionably Dr. Seuss was a talented and forward thinking man (but I'm glad that he isn't alive to read my filthy literature)

Finally I have to acknowledge anyone who has spoken, written or taken action to try to influence abortion laws, public opinion or both, without whom this book would not be possible. The fact that this controversy has been fought for literally 1000s of years exemplifies that what has been shall be, and what has been done will be done again.

Brandon "Thvndar" Sindos was born in New York City and raised in Westchester county as a third generation resident of New Rochelle, NY. He has been writing since 2009.

Facebook.com/Thvndar

@THVNDAR

Youtube.com/Thvndar

"If [my daughters] made a mistake, I don't want them punished with a baby"
- Barack Obama

"I've noticed that everyone who is for abortion has already been born."
- Ronald Reagan

www.ingramcontent.com/pod-product-compliance
Lightning Source LLC
Chambersburg PA
CBHW040129270326
41927CB00004B/94